I hope you can FEEL God's love for you— how PERSONALLY He takes caring for every detail of your life. I am asking Him to overwhelm you with LOVE and hopefulness today.

God is faithful, by whom you were c[c]
into the fellowship of his Son,
Jesus Christ our Lord.

1 CORINTHIANS 1:9 ESV

Because God is faithful, He can
trusted fully to completely carr
His commitments to us.

Jimmy Swaggart

DaySpring

There's no better place to invest
your energy than in
knowing God
and trusting His heart for you.
I am praying that as you
draw near to Him, you'll feel
His close presence and love.

*You will keep in perfect peace
those whose minds are steadfast,
because they trust in You.*
ISAIAH 26:3 NIV

If God was faithful to you yesterday,
you have reason to trust him
for tomorrow.
Woodrow Kroll

All we need is God's overwhelming love, constant care, and perfect peace. May you sense them all today.

May the God of hope fill you with all joy and peace in believing, so that you will abound in hope by the power of the Holy Spirit.

ROMANS 15:13 NASB

We cannot always trace God's hand, but we can always trust God's heart.

CHARLES SPURGEON

*Praying that God
blesses you with
your heart's desires
as you seek
His guidance.*

Take delight in the LORD, and He will
give you your heart's desires.
Commit everything you do to the LORD.
Trust Him, and He will help you.

PSALM 37:4–5 NLT

*Trust is not a belief that God
can bless or that He will bless,
but that He does bless, here and now.*

E. M. BOUNDS

$\mathcal{W}$hat an adventure life can be
with Jesus as your guide!
Asking Him to hold your hand tight
as He guides you one step at a time.

*The LORD is my shepherd,
I lack nothing.*

PSALM 23:1 NIV

God won't light your second step
until you have taken the first one.

WOODROW KROLL

As you pray, may perfect *peace* fill you. And may *joy* ignite your *passion* to look to tomorrow with anticipation and hope.

Rejoice always, pray without ceasing,
in everything give thanks; for this is
the will of God for you in Christ Jesus.

1 THESSALONIANS 5:16–18 NASB

Prayer is the most tangible expression
of trust in God.

JERRY BRIDGES

One foot FEARLESSLY in front of the other. That's how you're going FORWARD. And I'm praying that God wraps His LOVE around you with purpose and peace!

Such love has no fear, because perfect love expels all fear.

I JOHN 4:18 NLT

Faith wouldn't be faith without having to trust what is unseen. That's difficult sometimes, and it's almost easier to put our trust in what is tangible. But God wants us to put one foot in front of the other and just step out on faith.

Rebecca St. James

DaySpring

What a miracle of grace
and peace you are. I'm praying
you can see just a piece
of how you bless the world today
and feel power God has given you!

With the power of God within us,
we need never fear the powers
around us.

Woodrow Kroll

I'm praying God will strengthen your spirit, and make you an ambassador of His peace.

Peace I leave with you,
My peace I give to you.
JOHN 14:27 NKJV

A great many people are trying to make peace, but that has already been done. God has not left it for us to do; all we have to do— is to enter into it.

KATHERINE WALDEN

DaySpring

It's easy when we can see where we're going, and scary when the road is dark. But when faith steps in, your steps can be sure and you can be excited about what's to come! I'm praying that your faith conquers your fear.

Now faith is confidence in what we hope for and assurance about what we do not see.
HEBREWS 11:1 NIV

Meet your fears with faith.
MAX LUCADO

The Father loves you, and even now He is providing for you. He knows your needs, and He has already determined that He will meet them. As you wait for His perfect timing, I am praying you know beyond all else that *you are loved.*

We know how dearly God loves us, because He has given us the Holy Spirit to fill our hearts with His love.

ROMANS 5:5 NLT

Love is a roof that absorbs the storms.

ANN VOSKAMP

I am asking God to bring important *truth* to your mind when you need it most. May His voice be your *comfort,* all day long.

The LORD's voice is powerful;
the LORD's voice is majestic.

PSALM 29:4 NCV

When you take time with God and listen to His voice, He renews your strength and enables you to handle life.

JOYCE MEYER

DaySpring

May God use every tear and trial to build you up, give you WISDOM and COURAGE, and lead you to others who need the gifts of LOVE and ENCOURAGEMENT that only you have.

The Father of compassion and the God of all comfort...comforts us in all our troubles, so that we can comfort those in any trouble with the comfort we ourselves receive from God.

II CORINTHIANS 1:3–4 NIV

I would go to the deeps a hundred times to cheer a downcast spirit. It is good for me to have been afflicted, that I might know how to speak a word in season to one that is weary.

Charles Spurgeon

DaySpring

There's nothing to fear
when God is near.

Stay strong.

I'll keep praying things
will shine more brightly soon.

God knows our situation;
He will not judge us as if we had
no difficulties to overcome. What matters
is the sincerity and perseverance
of our will to overcome them.

C. S. Lewis

When life gets crazy,
I hope you know, you've got
a God who loves you so.
I'm praying His presence is close
and comforting for you!

I am the God of your father Abraham;
do not fear, for I am with you. I will bless you.
GENESIS 26:24 NKJV

When the news of the day upsets me,
I pause and worship the eternal
sovereign God who is never surprised
or caught unprepared. This keeps me
from fretting and getting discouraged,
and it helps to keep my life in balance.

KATHERINE WALDEN

DaySpring

*You've got all the tools
you need to make
this day amazing.
Praying!*

Thank You for making me
so wonderfully complex!
Your workmanship is marvelous—
how well I know it.

PSALM 139:14 NLT

*When we're bombarded with doubts
and fears, we must take a stand and say:
"I'll never give up! God's on my side.
He loves me, and He's helping me!
I'm going to make it!"*

JOYCE MEYER

*P*eace comes from the inside out.
And today, I'm asking God to fill you
with such a sense of peace
that everyone around you
can feel it, too.

But I have calmed and quieted my soul,
like a weaned child with its mother;
like a weaned child is my soul within me.

PSALM 131:2 ESV

Real contentment must come from within. You and I
cannot change or control the world around us,
but we can change and control the world within us.

WARREN WIERSBE

DaySpring

It's not unusual to feel alone
in challenging times. May you know
in your deepest *spirit* that God
is with you and that many
are *praying*. I'm here
as much as you need.

Jesus often slipped away to be alone
so He could pray.

LUKE 5:16 NCV

If I could hear Christ praying for me
in the next room, I would not fear
a million enemies. Yet distance makes
no difference. He is praying for me.

ROBERT MURRAY McCHEYNE

DaySpring

God says that when we ask for WISDOM He will give it. I will pray, TODAY and every day, for EXACTLY the wisdom you need.

Do not forsake wisdom, and she will protect you; love her, and she will watch over you.

PROVERBS 4:6 NIV

It is impossible to quarrel with someone who is filled with God's wisdom, for such a person is a peaceable person.

Zac Poonen

DaySpring

May your thoughts easily drift
toward all the good things
going for you, and may God's love
keep you feeling connected
and cared for in every way.

*Those who love Your teachings will find true peace,
and nothing will defeat them.*

PSALM 119:165 NCV

Concentrate on counting your blessings
and you'll have little time to count
anything else.

Woodrow Kroll

DaySpring

I'm praying you feel as blessed
as you make others feel
with your sweet smile
and kind heart.

A gentle answer will calm a person's anger,
but an unkind answer will cause more anger.

PROVERBS 15:1 NCV

Peace begins with a smile.

MOTHER TERESA

DaySpring

As you step out in faith,
God will step in
to walk alongside you,
encourage you,
and strengthen you
for the journey.
Praying for you!

Jesus said, "Come." And Peter left the boat
and walked on the water to Jesus.

MATTHEW 14:29 NCV

No circumstance is so big
that He cannot control it.

JERRY BRIDGES

$\mathcal{N}$o matter what you're
going through, you're not alone.
I'm praying that you feel
my prayers for you today.

Even though I walk through the darkest valley,
I will fear no evil, for You are with me;
Your rod and Your staff, they comfort me.

PSALM 23:4 NIV

The world can create trouble in peace,
but God can create peace in trouble.

THOMAS WATSON

One *step* at a time,
one *day* at a time,
with God taking the lead,
you will *enter* into
His peaceful places.
Praying that for you.

Seek first His kingdom and His righteousness,
and all these things will be given to you as well.

MATTHEW 6:33 NIV

We must do our business faithfully;
without trouble or disquiet, recalling our
mind to God mildly, and with tranquility,
as often as we find it wandering from Him.

BROTHER LAWRENCE

DaySpring

You have a way of bringing COMFORT *and* PEACE *wherever you go. I'm asking God to* STRENGTHEN *your own peaceful heart today, and to help you make a difference along the way.*

Make every effort to keep yourselves united in the Spirit, binding yourselves together with peace.

EPHESIANS 4:3 NLT

Remember as you go about your day that you may be the only Jesus some of your friends, neighbors, and family will ever see.

Wanda E. Brunstetter

DaySpring

God's timing isn't always
easy to understand, but we can
trust that it is truly perfect.
I'm praying with you
and trusting He'll make it all
turn out just right.

For everything there is a season,
a time for every activity under heaven.

ECCLESIASTES 3:1 NLT

God is more than able to guide you
in the right path. Keep trusting Him.

Lailah Gifty Akita

You feel like your strength is small, but it's not. It's BIG. World-changing big. Make-it-over-that-mountain big. Big enough for you to do what you need to do. Because your strength is as big as the God in you. I am believing in you, praying with you.

He fills my life with good things.
PSALM 103:5 NLT

There are times that we trust God because of what we can see, but there are also times when we have to trust God in spite of what we see.

CHRISTINE CAINE

DaySpring

Hey, you...yep, you. The one feeling a little weary. Carrying that load. Fighting this battle. You're beautiful, you know that? It's true. And you can do this with Him. I'm standing with you in prayer!

Anyone who believes in Me may come and drink! For the Scriptures declare, "Rivers of living water will flow from his heart."

JOHN 7:38 NLT

Jesus tends to his people individually. He personally sees to our needs. We all receive Jesus' touch. We experience his care.

MAX LUCADO

Sometimes it seems as if *silence* is heaven's only answer. But lean close enough into that silence and you'll hear a *heartbeat* within it: Love. Love. Love. His *love* never changes. I pray you feel it today.

Jesus Christ is the same yesterday and today and forever.

HEBREWS 13:8 ESV

He said "Love...as I have loved you." We cannot love too much.

AMY CARMICHAEL

DaySpring

Good news:
there's really no such thing
as impossible for you because
all things are possible
with God. I am praying you feel
the reality of that today!

Trust in the LORD and do good.

PSALM 37:3 NLT

True faith means holding nothing back.
It means putting every hope
in God's fidelity to His promises.

Francis Chan

DaySpring

Being the best you can be ministers to others. You do that so well. I am praying that your example inspires those around you today.

In speech, conduct, love, faith, and purity, show yourself an example of those who believe.
I TIMOTHY 4:12 NASB

The Christian shoemaker does his duty not by putting little crosses on the shoes but by making good shoes, because God is interested in good craftsmanship.

MARTIN LUTHER

DaySpring

*Praying you'll experience
the fullness of His promises
as you walk close to His heart
and follow in His ways.*

"By His power we live and move and exist."
Some of your own poets have said:
"For we are His children."

ACTS 17:28 NCV

*We may speak about a place where there
are no tears, no death, no fear, no night;
but those are just the benefits of heaven.
The beauty of heaven is seeing God.*

MAX LUCADO

DaySpring

$\mathcal{I}$ am praying that you will
trust God and hide in His love.
May His refuge give you
the strength you need.

*Trust in Him at all times. Pour out your heart
to Him, for God is our refuge.*

PSALM 62:8 NLT

At my lowest, God is my hope.
At my weakest, God is my strength.
At my saddest, God is my comforter.

UNKNOWN

DaySpring

Praying your day is full of the good stuff, the really good stuff— *blessings* that make your heart happy, *memories* that bring you joy, and the *contentment* from God that refreshes your soul.

Your goodness and unfailing love
will pursue me all the days of my life.

PSALM 23:6 NLT

What you are is God's gift to you,
what you become is your gift to God.

HANS URS VON BALTHASAR

DaySpring

As you go through your day in your typical way, REMEMBER you're on somebody's mind, someone who is PRAYING you'll find precious BLESSINGS wherever you go.

Nothing can ever separate us from God's love... neither our fears for today nor our worries about tomorrow.

ROMANS 8:38 NLT

There is not a single thing that Jesus cannot change, control, and conquer because He is the living Lord.

Franklin Graham

DaySpring

When I think of someone
truly great, I think of you.
Today I've prayed in gratitude
for all He's doing
in and through you, and for
the ways He's fulfilling
His purposes and plans.

*You can make many plans,
but the LORD's purpose will prevail.*
PROVERBS 19:21 NLT

Faith is a thing of the mind. If you
do not believe that God is in control
and has formed you for a purpose,
then you will flounder on the high seas
of purposelessness.

Ravi Zacharias

You continue to make a difference in the lives you touch. Praying God will multiply the influence you're having in His kingdom.

They share freely and give generously to those in need. Their good deeds will be remembered forever. They will have influence and honor.

PSALM 112:9 NLT

The will of God will not take us where the grace of God cannot sustain us.

BILLY GRAHAM

There isn't a moment, a place, or a circumstance when God isn't right where you are— with love to hold you, strength to keep you, and hope to carry you through. Praying you know you're in His thoughts, His heart, and His care.

Nothing can ever separate us from God's love.
ROMANS 8:38 NLT

God is able to take the mess of our past and turn it into a message. He takes the trials and tests and turns them into a testimony.
CHRISTINE CAINE

DaySpring

*W*e've seen before what God can do, how He can make a way. His plans for us are beyond what we can imagine, and somehow, someway there's more joy to come! Praying with you for daily miracles and joy along the journey.

The mind of a person plans his way, but the LORD directs his steps.

PROVERBS 16:9 NASB

Faith does not eliminate questions.
But faith knows where to take them.

ELISABETH ELLIOT

No one knows what the future holds.
But we know *who* holds us.
We can *trust* that it will be good—
even when we don't know the details,
even when things turn out different
than we expect. Praying with you that
He'll *work* everything out amazingly.

Remember that I commanded you to be strong
and brave. Don't be afraid, because the LORD
your God will be with you everywhere you go.

JOSHUA 1:9 NCV

We are all faced with a series
of great opportunities brilliantly disguised
as impossible situations.

CHUCK SWINDOLL

DaySpring

I'm THINKING *of you today—* PRAYING *that every moment is alive with His* BLESSING *and guidance.*

"For I know the plans I have for you," says the LORD. "They are plans for good and not for disaster, to give you a future and a hope."

JEREMIAH 29:11 NLT

This is our time on the history line of God. This is it. What will we do with the one deep exhale of God on this earth? For we are but a vapor and we have to make it count. We're on. Direct us, Lord, and get us on our feet.

Beth Moore

It's hard to dream big dreams
and really believe they will come true.
The small dreams we can handle,
but the big ones? Not so much...
Until we remember that we've got
a great big God whose specialty
is making big dreams
made in Him come true. I'm praying with
you for your wildest dreams to come true.

*God can do anything, you know—far more than you could
ever imagine or guess or request in your wildest dreams!*

EPHESIANS 3:20 THE MESSAGE

Relying on God has to start all over
every day, as if nothing
has yet been done.

C. S. Lewis

DaySpring

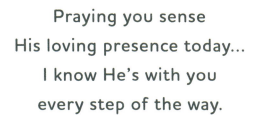

Praying you sense
His loving presence today...
I know He's with you
every step of the way.

*Let your good deeds shine out for all to see,
so that everyone will praise
your heavenly Father.*

MATTHEW 5:16 NLT

Let God's promises
shine on your problems.

CORRIE TEN BOOM

DaySpring

*I am praying you feel
the freedom of His perfect plan
for your life today, His guidance
of your every moment,
and His perfect plan
organizing each thought
into a beautiful pattern
of peace and joy.*

If you are faithful in little things,
you will be faithful in large ones.
LUKE 16:10 NLT

*There is no one who is insignificant
in the purpose of God.*
ALISTAIR BEGG

DaySpring

Today, I prayed you would know,
without a doubt, that you are
enough. Because He is enough.
And together, you are
more than enough for anything
that comes your way.

Whoever abides in me and I in him,
he it is that bears much fruit,
for apart from me you can do nothing.

JOHN 15:5 ESV

If God is your partner, make your plans BIG!

D. L. MOODY

Today, I prayed that you would draw courage from *laughter* and *smiles*. Let's be *flexible* and not take ourselves—our schedules, plans, and expectations—too seriously.

The joy of the LORD is your strength.
NEHEMIAH 8:10 NKJV

If you believe in a God who controls the big things, you have to believe in a God who controls the little things. It is we, of course, to whom things look "little" or "big."

ELISABETH ELLIOT

God is the very best Dad there is—one who SUPPORTS you, ENCOURAGES you, and HELPS you along the way. I am praying you feel close to your heavenly Dad today!

You know me inside and out...
You know exactly how I was made.
PSALM 139:15 THE MESSAGE

Remember who you are.
Don't compromise for anyone,
for any reason. You are a child
of the Almighty God. Live that truth.
Lysa Terkeurst

Today doesn't have to be perfect.
Just make adjustments from yesterday
and keep on going. May God supply

*everything you need
to keep going.*

God's work done in God's way
will never lack God's supplies.

Hudson Taylor

Relying on the promise of God's love is what gives us courage. Praying that with each day that passes you will find your strength and your unique identity.

Live a life filled with love, following the example of Christ.
EPHESIANS 5:2 NLT

God loves each of us as if there were only one of us.

AUGUSTINE

DaySpring

Isn't it good to know that
the One you are trusting
to lead you is the One
who knows where you are going
and how to get you there?
I'm praying that as He directs
your steps, you are strong
in the knowledge that
He'll lead you into
all the right places.

Do not be afraid, for I am with you
and will bless you.
GENESIS 26:24 NLT

God will meet you where you are in order
to take you where He wants you to go.
TONY EVANS

Today I asked God

to build you up in Him—

refining, defining,

and *drawing* you in,

so that you know Him more

as you grow and reflect His love.

Work with enthusiasm, as though
you were working for the Lord
rather than for people.

EPHESIANS 6:7 NLT

It's about fully experiencing God's love
and letting it perfect you. It's not about
being somebody you are not. It's about
becoming who you really are.

STORMIE OMARTIAN

God gives love, because God is love! I am praying you're resting in His love today, even as you shower others with your love for them.

God arms me with strength, and He makes my way perfect.
PSALM 18:32 NLT

When your soul is resting,
your emotions are okay,
your mind is okay, and your will
is at peace with God,
not resisting what He's doing.

Joyce Meyer

I'm praying you know in the
deepest places of your heart
that you have a place in God's plan
that no one else can fill.
Your life is overflowing blessings
that only He can give!

You know that the LORD has chosen for Himself
those who are loyal to Him.
The LORD listens when I pray to Him.
PSALM 4:3 NCV

I have held many things in my hands,
and I have lost them all;
but whatever I have placed
in God's hands, that I still possess.

Martin Luther

DaySpring

Praying you'll sense God's love
in a special way and know
He's close by your side—
walking with you today and always.

I will walk among you; I will be your God,
and you will be My people.
LEVITICUS 26:12 NLT

God uses circumstances to help us be
the person we can be, the person He
wants us to be. He loves us just as we are,
of course, but He also uses the details
of our life to grow in strength and wisdom
and holiness. We are on a journey.

RACHEL SWENSON BALDUCCIE

DaySpring

My prayer for you is that you'll always have hope beyond your understanding. Something that carries you beyond circumstances and into joy unspeakable.

Though now you do not see Him, yet believing, you rejoice with joy inexpressible and full of glory, receiving the end of your faith.

1 PETER 1:8 NKJV

God cannot give us a happiness and peace apart from Himself, because it is not there. There is no such thing.

C. S. LEWIS

DaySpring

*E*very morning when you wake up,
may you open the closet
of your heart to find a wardrobe
of grace for you to choose from.
And may your covering of His love
grace every corner of your home.

Throw yourselves into the work of the Master,
confident that nothing you do for Him
is a waste of time or effort.

I CORINTHIANS 15:58 THE MESSAGE

I am not what I ought to be. I am not what I want to be.
I am not what I hope to be. But still, I am not what
I used to be. And by the grace of God, I am what I am.

JOHN NEWTON

DaySpring

God is the only one who can turn
scars into *beauty marks*.
May every experience meant to harm
become the *history* that shaped you
into the most loving, giving,
caring human possible.

Let your light shine for all to see.
For the glory of the LORD rises to shine on you.

ISAIAH 60:1 NLT

We are told to let our light shine,
and if it does, we won't need to
tell anybody it does. Lighthouses don't
fire cannons to call attention
to the shining—just shine.

DWIGHT L. MOODY

DaySpring

As you walk with Him,
you're NEVER alone.
He's ALWAYS with you,
and He will meet
your every need.
He cares about EVERY
step you take. So do I—
which is why I'm
praying for you often!

*God is my helper; the Lord
is the sustainer of my soul.*

PSALM 54:4 NASB

You are loved. More than you know.
More than you see. More than you've even
dared to dream. We can stop doubting.
We can be secure in love.

Holley Gerth

May His tenderness toward you

be the strength you need

to carry His light throughout
your day—because you are
a true gift to your family,
your friends, and the world.

*We never give up....
Our Spirits are being renewed every day.*

II CORINTHIANS 4:16 NLT

Happiness always looks small
while you hold it in your hands,
but let it go, and you learn at once
how big and precious it is.

Maxim Gorky

DaySpring

Where you can't concentrate,
God is more than focused enough.
I'm asking Him to use your strengths,
fill your gaps, and steer you
through the details of today.

*Give all your worries and cares to God,
for He cares about you.*
1 PETER 5:7 NLT

Our lives hold no details too small
for God's care and attention.
If the Lord cares enough to count
the hairs on our heads,
He cares enough to steer
our smaller, day-to-day choices.

KRISTIN SMITH

DaySpring

*Praying that the God of peace
would fill your heart
with all the peace you need,
today and every day.*

And the peace of God, which transcends
all understanding, will guard your hearts
and your minds in Christ Jesus.

PHILIPPIANS 4:7 NIV

*The moment you wake up each morning,
all your wishes and hopes for the day
rush at you like wild animals. And the first job
each morning consists in shoving it all back;
in listening to that other voice, taking that
other point of view, letting that other, larger,
stronger, quieter life come flowing in.*

C. S. LEWIS

I am asking God to meet you in the everyday, with all the joy, patience, and grace you need to thrive!

We also pray that you will be strengthened with all His glorious power so you will have all the endurance and patience you need. May you be filled with joy.

COLOSSIANS 1:11 NLT

You breathe different in a room when you know it's not about the good you can accomplish but about the grace you can accept.

ANN VOSKAMP

DaySpring

Do you know how *amazing* you are? Do you know you are prayed for and *loved* every single day? I hope so!

Come to Me, all who are weary and burdened, and I will give you rest.

MATTHEW 11:28 NASB

When we find we can't make a place for ourselves in this world, Jesus gently whispers, "Come here. Collapse into My arms. You can always stay here. You don't have to go anywhere. I am your place. Here. With Me. This way. Forever."

SATCHEL PAIGE

Thank You, God, for the **MERCY** we will never fully comprehend. Thank You for the **GRACE** we don't even know we need. Thank You for the **LOVE** that allows us to lift others up even as you lift us, grow us, and train us to follow Your lead.

You will show me the path of life;
in Your presence is fullness of joy;
at Your right hand are pleasures forevermore.
PSALM 16:11 NKJV

God loves us; not because we are lovable but because He is love, not because He needs to receive but because He delights to give.

C. S. Lewis

With God, all things are possible.

*Even forgiving
the unforgivable,*

loving the difficult...
and cleaning grape juice stains
out of carpet.

*Love...believes all things, hopes all things,
endures all things. Love never fails.*

I CORINTHIANS 13:4, 7–8 NASB

Try and fail. Try and succeed.
But always try. We don't know
what we're capable of unless we try.

Bianca Juarez Olthoff

DaySpring

Today, I prayed that a silent moment or two won't be hard to come by. That you'll enjoy peace in His presence and rest for your soul.

Let my soul be at rest again,
for the LORD has been good to me.

PSALM 116:7 NLT

I have held many things in my hands, and I have lost them all; but whatever I have placed in God's hands, that I still possess.

MARTIN LUTHER

DaySpring

Praying you can find joy
in the ordinary, even as you
rejoice in the extraordinary.
Praying you experience
generosity and love
in your everyday life.

As those who have been chosen of God,
holy and beloved, put on a heart of compassion,
kindness, humility, gentleness and patience....
In addition to all these things put on love,
which is the perfect bond of unity.
COLOSSIANS 3:12–14 NASB

We make a living by what we get,
but we make a life by what we give.
WINSTON CHURCHILL

DaySpring

You're in such good hands. I pray you sense how covered you are by His loving presence, even as you're giving all you've got, all day long.

He has given each one of us a special gift through the generosity of Christ.

EPHESIANS 4:7 NLT

You may not be able to see the difference that you're making, the lives you're touching, the joy you're bringing. But it's there. It's real. It's truer than true. So sit at that table with Jesus. Do what He says. Give Him your life and hold nothing back.

HOLLEY GERTH

DaySpring

God teaches us so much through the *vulnerability* and *gentleness* of a baby. May you find a place of *sweetness* and *protection* with your Father in heaven, knowing how much He loves you and cares for you.

If you go the wrong way—to the right or to the left—you will hear a voice behind you saying, "This is the right way. You should go this way."

ISAIAH 30:21 NCV

God possesses infinite knowledge and an awareness which is uniquely His. At all times...I can realize that He knows, loves, watches, understands, and more than that, He has a purpose.

BILLY GRAHAM

DaySpring

Sometimes stuff is just hard. Today I'm asking God to show you His CARE, COMFORT, and HOPE. I'm asking Him to do in your life what only He can do.

Which of you by worrying can add a single day to his life's span?

MATTHEW 6:27 NASB

His story is being told through my life; only in Christ's presence am I capable of rejoicing always despite circumstance, and that's the story I so long to share.

Robin Dance

Because of God's grace,
life can be peaceful and fun.
There's hope in Jesus
and I'm praying that hope
will overtake your daily life
in ways you can't even expect.

Let your light shine for all to see.
For the glory of the LORD rises to shine on you.
ISAIAH 60:1 NLT

What God has placed within you,
He wants to bring out of you.

Emily Freeman

DaySpring

Life can be hard, but you are such a good example. Praying for grace to overflow in your heart and hope to spill all over your circumstances today.

You will keep in perfect peace all who trust in You, all whose thoughts are fixed on You!
ISAIAH 26:3 NLT

To believe that God can reach us and bless us in the ordinary junctures of daily life is the stuff of prayer. You see, the only place God can bless us is right where we are, because that is the only place we are!

RICHARD J. FOSTER

*I stopped today to ask God
to bring miracles into your life,
to answer your prayers
in tangible ways, and to infuse
your home with more joy
than your heart can hold.*

Tell me in the morning about Your love,
because I trust You. Show me what I should do,
because my prayers go up to You.

PSALM 143:8 NCV

*My morning routine has changed. Instead of
waking up asking for things, nervous about
the day, trying to control my circumstances
with rapid gunfire prayers toward heaven,
I turn my heart toward grateful.
I acknowledge the small that can
break my day or make my attitude.*

STEPHANIE BRYANT

You are a light to everyone who knows you. I am praying your strength, confidence, and everything that makes you beautiful shines brightly today.

Those who wait for the LORD will gain new strength;
they will mount up with wings like eagles,
they will run and not get tired,
they will walk and not become weary.

ISAIAH 40:31 NASB

God chose me. He loves me. I wasn't a perfect and smooth rock when He found me—I was broken and cracked...yet He still thought I was beautiful.

AMANDA LEDFORD

DaySpring

Some days you feel you won't get through. For those days especially, know that I'm praying for His *extravagant, enthusiastic, generous* love to pour over you and cover your multitude of needs.

Don't worry about anything; instead, pray about everything.

PHILIPPIANS 4:6 NLT

The very best place you can ever be is in the center of God's will.

SUSAN GESELL

DaySpring

Thank You, Jesus, for Your peace. Thank You for Your daily hope. Thank You for blessing us with glory-to-glory riches as we walk through each day with You.

I press on toward the goal for the prize of the upward call of God in Christ Jesus.

PHILIPPIANS 3:14 NASB

Good news for today: God is still in charge
and in control! He is beside you,
behind you, before you, and for you!
No doubt about it, no way around it—
His plan is good, His power is great,
and His best is yet to come!

Matt Anderson

DaySpring

Life is overflowing with God's goodness...
including the blessing of you.
It may not always feel like it—but who
you are really makes a difference
to your family, community, and the world.
I pray you feel the reality of that today!

The LORD will continually guide you, and satisfy
your desire in scorched places, and give strength
to your bones; and you will be like a watered garden,
and like a spring of water whose waters do not fail.

ISAIAH 58:11 NASB

You don't have to watch
the weather patterns to know
the One who controls them.
You just have to believe He does.

Angie Smith

DaySpring

I prayed for you to experience the fullness of God's blessings in your life so you can't help but to live in constant wonder and thankfulness.

How kind the LORD is! How good He is!
PSALM 116:5 NLT

Don't cry over things that were
or things that aren't.
Enjoy what you have now
to the fullest.

BARBARA BUSH

DaySpring

*You are so equipped to do
this life with amazing excellence.
I'm praying you see how
the time and love you invest
every day makes a big difference.*

Let us run with endurance the race
God has set before us. We do this
by keeping our eyes on Jesus,
the champion who initiates
and perfects our faith.

HEBREWS 12:1–2 NLT

*We grow in this great life
by making room for Jesus Christ
in our outlook on everything.*

OSWALD CHAMBERS

*M*ay God give you His mercy so fully that you have no choice but to let love burst out of you. Every day.

The LORD is good to everyone;
He is merciful to all He has made.

PSALM 145:9 NCV

There's nothing that falls just outside of what was nailed to the cross. God isn't up there thinking, "Oh crud, she did that?! Because I didn't make provisions for that... now what am I going to do with her? I guess she'll just have to live with the guilt." Uh-uh, all of sin was taken out. All of your sin was covered over. Even that really, really bad thing you did.

ELISABETH CORCORAN

Today I prayed that you
would see yourself the way
God *sees you*. He loves you
and *delights* in watching
your life unfold.

He said to me, "My grace is enough for you.
When you are weak, My power
is made perfect in you."

II CORINTHIANS 12:9 NCV

God exists now. God says "I Am."
Not "I Was" or "I Will Be" or "I'll Be Ready
for You When You Get that Thing You Want."
He is, now, always.

MARIA BAER

What a RELIEF to realize He's not asking us to be perfect! My PRAYER for you is that His incredible GRACE fills your every moment, no matter how that moment turns out, that you follow His will, wherever that takes you.

The moment I called out, You stepped in; You made my life large with strength.
PSALM 138:3 THE MESSAGE

That's the thing about God— when we offer our dreams to Him, He makes us want to do His will.

Jamie Martin

Today I'm thanking God for
pouring His goodness
on you. I'm asking Him
to bless you with more
of Himself—His presence,
His peace, and His joy!

*My God will use His wonderful riches in Christ Jesus
to give you everything you need.*
PHILIPPIANS 4:19 NCV

The best way to tend to your
open wounds is to open your arms.
Out-loving is the only ointment
that healed anything.

Ann Voskamp

DaySpring

Today, I asked God to infuse you with His strength and courage, to work in you so you can dream big. There's nothing you can't do with Him in you!

In all the work you are doing, work the best you can. Work as if you were doing it for the Lord, not for people.

COLOSSIANS 3:23 NCV

What happens in us matters far more than what happens to us. Our experiences don't define us; our response to them does.

ALECE RONZINO

DaySpring

May God give you grace
for everyday challenges
and abiding love for all
the moments when your heart
needs strength. I'm praying
His love will meet you
in a quiet place today
and refresh you completely.

The LORD rewarded me for doing right.
He has seen my innocence.

PSALM 18:24 NLT

Exhale a little and think about failure
being God's gift of redirection.

TRACEE PERSIKO

DaySpring

My prayer for you is that you see the care with which God keeps watch over you. I pray that as He loves you, you will love others with the same extravagance.

We love, because He first loved us.

I JOHN 4:19 NASB

There is a time for risky love. There is a time for extravagant gestures. There is a time to pour out your affections on the one you love. And when the time comes—seize it, don't miss it.

MAX LUCADO

Holding onto *Jesus* is the very best way to make it through. That's why I'm *praying* for you—to feel His arms around you, His gentle *whisper* in your ear as you go along this beautiful journey of life.

Blessed be the God and Father
of our Lord Jesus Christ, who has blessed us
with every spiritual blessing
in the heavenly places in Christ.

EPHESIANS 1:3 NASB

Happiness is being at peace,
being with loved ones, being comfortable....
But most of all, it's having those loved ones.

JOHNNY CASH

I want you to REMEMBER that you're KNOWN by the Creator of the universe. He PICKED you for such a time as this. No one in this world can do "you" better than you can. Just wait.

Strength and dignity are her clothing, and she smiles at the future.

PROVERBS 31:25 NASB

A wise gardener plants his seeds, then has the good sense not to dig them up every few days to see if a crop is on the way. Likewise, we must be patient as God brings the answers...in His own good time.

Quin Sherrer

Oh friend, I pray you know how *special you are to God,* how often His thoughts go to you. What an asset you are to your family. How needed you are in this world. I thank God for you.

God, Your thoughts are precious to me. They are so many!

PSALM 139:17 NCV

Help me, Jesus, to never stop learning what You are teaching.

Stacey Thacker

DaySpring

Your hopes and dreams matter
to God—truly! I've asked Him
to lead you in the fulfillment
of all of your wildest desires,
even if you have to start again.

God doesn't miss anything. He knows
perfectly well all the love you've shown...
and that you keep at it.
HEBREWS 6:10 THE MESSAGE

God isn't disappointed in our failures;
He delights in our attempts.

BOB GOFF

There's no more important part of a day than when we turn to Jesus. I'm praying He helps arrange your time with as much grace as you need, blessing your day with special moments for prayer and closeness.

The LORD will fulfill his purpose for me;
your steadfast love, O LORD, endures forever.
PSALM 138:8 ESV

Never give up.... Find another way.
And don't pray when it rains
if you don't pray when the sun shines.
SATCHEL PAIGE

*S*ometimes praying doesn't feel like enough—but it's always important to God! Today, I'm lifting you up and asking Him to make His answers very clear to you.

I will call to God for help, and the LORD will save me. Morning, noon, and night I am troubled and upset, but He will listen to me.

PSALM 55:16–17 NCV

Don't forget to remember, fear tells you who you are not, but faith reminds you who you are!

CHRISTINE CAINE

DaySpring

I'm so thankful we serve a God of the *impossible, impractical,* and *unforgivable*. I'm praying His unshakable, unchanging hope fills you with joy today.

As soon as I pray, You answer me;
You encourage me by giving me strength.

PSALM 138:3 NLT

There is no force on earth stronger
or more effective than the power of praying
to our all-knowing, almighty God.

LINN CARLSON

DaySpring

What a BEAUTIFUL soul and AMAZING person you are. I'm praying you know it, feel it, and live with the knowledge that you have been MOLDED by God.

By the grace of God I am what I am, and His grace toward me was not in vain.

I CORINTHIANS 15:10 NKJV

We are never given over to "random chance" by our Creator. He is conforming and molding us into His likeness.

Heather George

DaySpring

It's not always easy to love—
but God can do it
through us, in any situation.
Today I'm asking Him to give you
everything you need to be the love
others need. And for you to feel
His love for you.

Let us come boldly to the throne of our gracious God.
There we will receive His mercy, and we will find grace
to help us when we need it most.

HEBREWS 4:16 NLT

There isn't a certain time we should
set aside to talk about God. God is part
of our every waking moment.

Marva Collins

DaySpring